M White-Pritchard GDPR.cert

GDPR:

Website Wealth

Data Privacy Impact Assessment

Disclaimer

In Memoriam

Mamie Ruth White

Robbie Lee Jones

(1927-2016)

Contents

1   Introduction

2   Understanding GDPR p.2

3   Understand Your Data p.5

4   SWOT Analysis p.6

5   Strenghts p.9

6   Weaknesses p.16

7   Opportunities p.23

8   Threats p.35

9   Summary p.41

10   Preparing for GDPR p.43

11   The Rights p.44

12   The Seven Principles p.44

13   The GDPR Index of The Regulation p.46

14   References p.55

15   The Author p.56

GDPR: Website Wealth

Introduction

"People have a right to expect that when they share their personal information, it will be handled properly and legally. That is especially so when it is sensitive personal data." Steve Eckersley, ICO Head of Enforcement

"In the digital economy, data is very often the greatest asset a company has. But also,

their greatest detriment can be data – so if they're not treating it in accordance with the regulations and legal requirements, they're going to have massive problems."

Sheila Fitzpatrick [a world leading expert in data privacy laws]

Data is the life blood of all businesses. In today's wired world your website is an invaluable business tool. It can work 24/7 online and supply you with a 'shop window', marketing leads, customer information and sales. But what if almost overnight you were no longer able to access its benefits? What if your website stopped being a wealth generating asset and turned into a risk. A threat capable of imposing fines, penalties and challenging the continued existence of your website/business? Does this sound impossible? No, it is not. With the introduction of the General Data Protection Regulation (GDPR), a seismic shift will take place regarding how websites/businesses are required to comply with new data protection regulations for all EU citizens.

Understanding GDPR

From 25th May 2018, the General Data Protection Regulation (GDPR) will come into force. The GDPR will affect websites/businesses in their collection and processing of EU citizens' individual identifiable information. This requires a new understanding of people's data collection, usage and how it should be processed.

https://www.youtube.com/watch?v=WgVPylVy4sY&t=22s

In a nutshell GDPR is about:

Data inventory and its legal usage.

Policy, protocol and security measures.

Audit and data sharing validation and verification.

The General Data Protection Regulation (GDPR) has 99 Articles and 173 Recitals.

It has **strict rules** for the **handling** of EU citizens' data in regards to:

Collection

Hosting

Processing

Sharing

Penalties

Fines

It has **strict rules** on how **consent** is obtained/

permission options:

Opt-in and Opt-out

Right To Be Forgotten

Subject Access Request (SAR)

Rights for informing individuals

Use of data for sales and marketing purposes

How data subjects are informed of any issues regarding

the control and management of their data (i.e. breaches)

GDPR will affect different types of websites/businesses in

different ways. As a result, it may initially seem confusing

how best to shape your compliance strategy. If you are in

doubt then consider best practice. Consult only specialists who understand the implications and impact of GDPR for your specific industry; your designated authority/ Information Commissioner's Office (ICO) UK, legal counsel and/or a Certified GDPR Practitioner/ Data Protection Officer (DPO). You must get your compliance strategy right or risk getting everything wrong. Do not underestimate the importance of developing an informed strategy before you begin. One that can deliver GDPR compliance and meets all of your obligations under the regulation. It cannot be stressed enough to always remember that GDPR compliance is not a 'one size fits all' or 'just an IT project'. All departments should be involved in developing your GDPR strategy; legal, human resources, compliance, procurement, marketing and public relations. Since non-compliance is not an option, how you comply can be a deciding factor in whether your website/business will continue to 'live or die'.

Understand Your Data

How you collect it.

Why you hold it

What you do with it.

Where you store it.

How long you keep it.

How securely the data is kept.

It is also important to review all IT systems used to trace the data's journey.

http://www.legislation.gov.uk/ukpga/1998/29/contents

SWOT Analysis

GDPR requirements are weighted against the processes, procedures and values of your website/business in a consistent manner. The priorities and gaps you find will lay the foundation for your compliance strategy and will enable you to understand your sensitive data, its location, and application.

For clarity, I will use a SWOT Analysis i.e. [STRENGHT, WEAKNESS, OPPORTUNITY, THREAT] in association with the GDPR to help you assess your website/ business.

The SWOT Analysis can help:

Provide you with the necessary preliminary insight.

Assist you in creating a strategy that is viable and coherent.

Start your planning and compliance formulations.

The SWOT business analysis will highlight GDPR online practices to assist you in thinking about and developing your individual online compliance strategy.

It will assist you to begin analysing and addressing what procedures, protocols and systems you will need for Data Protection by Design.

Remember:

Be rigorous and realistic.

Use SWOT as a guide and not a recommendation.

http://www.legislation.gov.uk/ukpga/1998/29/contents

SWOT Analysis: Assessment Plan

Step 1 Information gathering – record all **Strengths** that currently exist.

Step 2 Information gathering - record all **Weaknesses** that currently exist.

Step 3 Record and analyse all **Opportunities** i.e. likely future strengths.

Step 4 Record and analyse all **Threats** you may encounter at some point.

Step 5 Action Plan – Make a plan for each step of the assessment.

Using the SWOT Analysis, answer each information point.

[YES] if the information is known **[NO]** if the information is unknown.

(Use the left hand margin of the SWOT to keep track of your answers)

http://www.fairdata.org.uk/why-fair-data/

STRENGHTS

Communication and Awareness:

Compliance with GDPR, The Human Rights Act 1998

The Privacy and Electronic Communication Regulation

(PECR) 2003

Amendment Regulations 2016

The Data Protection Bill 2017. ICO, _Direct Marketing_.

Compliance with the GDPR Data Protection Principles:

Processing of personal data

Lawfulness of processing

Conditions of consent processing of special categories of

personal data, and Processing that does not require

identification. Articles 5-11.

GDPR Rights of the data subject:

To Access

To Be Informed

To Rectification

To Erasure

To Portability

To Restricted Processing

To Objection

In Relation To Automated Decision Making And Profiling. Articles 12-22.

Building Privacy Controls into everything the business does.

Research the latest business developments that address data protection matters.

Consultation as recommended by Information Commission's Office (ICO). ICO, *Conducting PIA code of practice*.

External consultation provides an opportunity to get input from people who will be affected by the project and to benefit from wider experience. Article 35(9).

Consultation with internal experts can highlight privacy risks and solutions.

May improve confidence and transparency in the public's understanding of their data usage.

Promote accountability and governance that demonstrate compliance and understanding. Article 5(2). Establish cooperation with the supervisory authority. Article 31.

Insure that the business can demonstrate compliance and implement:

Comprehensive but <u>proportionate</u> governance measures.

Appropriate technical and policy measures to ensure compliance.

The use of **Data Protection Impact Assessments** where appropriate.

Data Protection By Design and Data Protection By Default includes:

Data Minimisation

Pseudonymisation

Transparency

Individuals being allowed to monitor processing.

Improving security features on an ongoing basis.

Safe processing activities on relevant documents and

their maintenance.

Compliance with approved codes of conduct and/or certification schemes.

Enlist a Data Protection Officer (DPO) to ensure compliance with GDPR, if it applies. Articles 37-39.

Appoint a Data Protection Officer (DPO) where appropriate:

To inform and advise the data controller and processor about their obligations under the GDPR.

Assist with the construction of policy and procedure framework.

Monitor compliance of the controller and processor.

Advise and provide consultation on the processing of large amounts of data and special categories of personal data.

Act as a liaison and a point of contact for Data Privacy Impact Assessment (PIA).

Implement a Data Privacy Impact Assessment (DPIA) Article 35.

This will set the requirements for privacy solutions that need to be implemented and balance privacy risks against business objectives. ICO, *Conducting PIA code of practice*.

In a nutshell you need to carry out a DPIA when:

Using new technologies to process data

Processing is likely to result in high risk to the rights and freedoms of

individuals e.g. based on the sensitivity of the processing activity.

DPIA information should contain:

Description of the processing operations and the purposes; including the legitimate interests pursued by the controller where applicable.

An assessment of the necessity and proportionality of the processing in relation to the purpose.

An assessment of the risks to individuals.

The measures in place to address risk, including security and to demonstrate compliance.

Risk-based approach to be adopted <u>before</u> starting any data inventory processing:

Identify what is right, affordable and relevant for your business.

Assist in describing data flow and how you plan to use It.

Identify privacy risks and needs of users.

Allow the introduction of specific goals for privacy controls.

Assess, plans and improve implementation of privacy solutions.

Help to identify privacy risks and needs of users.

Allow work to be done systematically to identify potential risks.

Facilitate the creation of customised templates, screening questions, and consultation methods.

Develop the standards all projects should be expected to meet.

Use automated systems that are devised to check against standard privacy risks/ Agile projects.

Include an element of how user needs are being met. This can help create valuable feedback to help you understand how privacy risks are arising.

The International Standard for Risk Management (ISO 31000) can provide comprehensive principles and guide lines to identify risks.

Identify privacy risks associated with anonymised personal data and sharing it with partners.

Clarify how information will be obtained, used, and retained.

Record privacy risks and solutions on a privacy risk register.

Identify who is responsible for approving and implementing the solution.

Explain what action has been taken or will be taken.

Establish standards for privacy all projects can be compared against.

Adhere to Codes of Conduct in your industry, with context specific rules that comply with GDPR.

WEAKNESSES

Lack of understanding, clarity and non-compliance

regarding the responsibilities and obligations under GDPR. ICO, *Overview of the GDPR*.

Failure to establish rights:

Lawfulness of processing. Article 6.

Conditions for consent. Article 7.

Special categories of personal data processing. Article 9.

Failure to identify risk:

No documentation of the origin, nature, and severity of the risk.

Unclear profile of the risks involved.

No risk assessment in regards to the rights and freedoms of data subjects.

No safeguards and security mechanisms to ensure risks can be identified.

Not defining the measures initiated to address the risks.

Unprotected personal data and compliance cannot be

demonstrated.

Failure to establish automated systems:

Capable of GDPR compliance, data retention, data processing with data sharing safeguards, data portability protocol, secure IT, encryption, and partnership safeguards. ICO, *Conducting PIA code of practice*. Designed to facilitate monitoring of automated systems, procedures and protocol for ongoing compliance.

Able to verify the work and secure the data processing.

Failure to establish legality:

There must be legally binding contracts with data processing partners that set out clear responsibilities for all concerned:

What

When

Where

How

By Whom

How Long the data is to be handled.

Note: The contracts must include all partners involved in security, IT, the retention policies and processes. Article 26.

All partners must be GDPR compliant for processing and data storage facilities.

Failure to establish an adequate budget for:

A GDPR project to cover all costs, including contingencies.

A Data Protection Officer (DPO), Articles 37-39. or appoint of a person who will be responsible for the data, assets and the Data Privacy Impact Assessment (PIA).

Failure to establish responsibilities and accountability for:

The Data Controller and Processor. Article 24-34.

A **Data Protection Impact Assessment** (DPIA). Article 35.

Failure to:

Use automated systems, processes, procedures and protocols for data handling.

Manage process, protocol and systems to monitor

compliance. Article 29.

Record processing activities accurately and adequately.

Article 30.

Maintain internal records of processing activities.

Provide the name and details of your business.

State the purposes of the processing.

Describe the categories of individuals, personal data and recipients of personal data.

Give details and documentation of transfers to third countries including mechanisms and safeguards.

Use retention schedules.

Supply a description of technical and business security measures.

Identify the type of data you process:

Classify and inventory data and assign risk protection profiles.

Show implementation of data security measures and verification of the work:

Where the data is stored?

Who is accountable for the data?

Who has access to the data?

Who is sharing the data?

What process is used to monitor data?

How is consent obtained, retained and removed?

Establish the right of access under GDPR. Article 15.

The GDPR allows data subjects the right to access and verify the lawfulness of processing of their personal data. Recital 63.

Create a system and procedure that can facilitate Subject Access Requests (SAR).

Train your staff in GDPR, data protection and how to do SAR.

Incorporate guidance for Subject Access Request (SAR):

Specify the information a requester will need to provide to confirm their identity.

Makes it clear where the request should be sent.

Mention the 30 day period for responding to the request.

Give details of a point of contact for any questions.

Train staff in GDPR data compliance that reflects up to date regulatory practices.

Select only GDPR compliant partners for processing and data storage facilities.

Provide data security safeguards and data sharing protocol (on computers, servers, in the cloud, personal mobile devices).

Create a disaster recovery plan, in case of breach.

Have adequate safeguards and controls in place to transfer data.

Make available contact details of your processor:

For Cloud usage or to store personal data with a supplier who uses Cloud services, they must comply with regulations for Transfer of Personal Data to third country or international organisations. Articles 44-50.

Cross boarder processing must be approved by the European Data Protection Board (the EDPB). The general principle for transfers is to prevent unauthorised data transfers outside member states for data processing, transfer, disclosure, and sharing.

OPPORTUNITIES

Create a system that is GDPR by Design and by Default, Article 25.

Security by Design – All automated systems and IT security should be designed secure to safeguard personal data rights and to reduce the risk of data breach. ICO, *Conducting PIA code if practice.*

Create an automated IT system for data collection that is fit for purpose to:

Collect, Access and Inform

Delete the data upon request

Change and Store the data

Provide Subject Access Requests (SAR)

Restrict and Transfer the data

Automate individual decision making, including profiling. Articles 12-22.

Establish Compliance and **Best Practice**

Certification is issued by supervisory authorities or accredited certification bodies.

Certification scheme or Codes of Conduct are approved by the Information Commission's Office (ICO). They are issued by supervisory authorities or accredited certification bodies and are not mandatory but can:

Validate certification for a maximum of three years

Improve transparency and accountability

Provide measures against mitigation and enforcement action

Help comply with the law

Act as a mitigating factor upon enforcement action

Topics cover by Codes of Conduct are:

Fair and transparent processing

Legitimate interests pursued by controllers in specific contexts:

Collection of personal data

Pseudonymisation of personal data

Information provided to individual and the exercise of individuals' rights

Information provided to and the protection of children

(including mechanisms for obtaining parental consent)

Technical and organisational measures (including data protection by design and by default and security measures)

Breach notification

Data transfer outside the EU

Dispute resolution procedures

Certification mechanism establishes compliance and demonstrates:

Implementation of technical and organisational measures

Existence of appropriate safeguards related to data transfers

How individuals are allowed to quickly assess the level of data protection of a particular product or service.

Use compliant Web Applications:

Data encryption

Firewall appliances

Secure connections to transmit data

Security vulnerabilities test

Malicious activity monitor

Establish GDPR Direct Marketing compliance. ICO, _Direct Marketing_. The Data Protection Act defines "direct marketing" as _"the communication (by whatever means) of any advertising or marketing material which is directed to particular individuals"_.

Marketing and promotion cover any contact with a named individual.

Universal Opt-out applies and Opt-out must not be made difficult to do. The Data Protection Act Opt-out terms still apply.

Data subjects have the right to object at any time. Article 21 (2,3).

Privacy and Electronic Communications (EC Directive) Regulation 2003 (PECR)

"Nothing in these Regulations shall relieve a person of his obligations under the Data Protection Act 1998 in relation to the processing of personal data." ICO, *Direct Marketing.*

PECR covers direct marketing made via:

Email

Phone

Text

Cookies

It requires the subject to notify the sender that consent is granted <u>before</u> the sender can contact the data subject. This applies to any calls, texts, or emails made for <u>any</u> direct marketing purpose, including lead generation (even if there is no promotional or sales material in the first message).

Consent should be the same standard as GDPR:

Free

Specific

Informed

Unambiguous

There is <u>no right</u> to send marketing to donors and customers.

Evidence of consent is needed from suppliers too.

Note: There are no restrictions on sending solicited marketing that the person has specifically requested.

The 'Cookie Law' is changed. The Directive on Privacy and Electronic Communications. Cookies are online identifiers and personal data. Recital 30.

Consent is required before placing Cookies on the data subject's computer.

Opt-in requires a data subject's <u>specific consent</u> before SMS/Text/Email can be sent.

An unticked box is <u>not</u> consent.

Asking existing contacts to provide contact details for their friends and family is <u>not</u> acceptable.

Opt-out must be made clear and not difficult to do. [Morrisons (2017, £10000 ICO MPN) & Flybe (2017, £10000 ICO MPN)]

Soft Opt-in is:

Marketing only similar products or services.

Data obtained in sale or negotiations for sale.

Data Protection Rights over marketing to include profiling.

An opportunity to Opt-out given at the time and in every subsequent message.

Privacy Policy

The Privacy Policy must explain clearly that you intend to use the details collected for marketing purposes. ICO, *Privacy notices, transparency and control*. It should consider adverse impacts and also include the data subject's

GDPR Rights:

To Be Informed

To Access

To Rectification

To Erasure

To Restrict Processing

To Data Portability

To Object

In Relation To Automated Decision Making And Profiling

(Articles 12-22)

GDPR Principles:

Principles relating to processing of personal data

Lawfulness of processing

Conditions of consent

Conditions applicable to child's consent in relation to

information society services

Processing of special categories of personal data

Processing of personal data relating to criminal

convictions and offences

Processing which does not require identification (Articles

5-11)

The **Privacy Policy** explains the purpose for the data

collection and must not be:

Concealed or misrepresented

Written in small print or be dense

Hidden away or lengthy

Unclear about any plans to sell or disclose data details

Unclear about how specific consent is obtained

Non-transparent in regards to:

Data rights

Processing procedure

Policies (including returns, refunds etc.)

Partner information

Cookies

Complaints procedure

Contact details for website/business

Contact details of Data Protection Officer (DPO)

Conditions of consent must be acknowledged

European Directive 95/46/EC **to use personal data for marketing or for use by others to be GDPR compliant.** ICO, *Direct Marketing.*

Non-targeted marketing (the same marketing displayed to every user)

Contextual marketing (targeted to the page itself rather than the identity or characteristics of users) is unlikely to be subject to the Data Protection Act.

Buying a Marketing List and GDPR. ICO, _Direct Marketing_.

The Data Protection Act 1998 requires that personal data held must be:

Adequate, relevant, and limited to what is necessary for processing.

Data should not be kept any longer than necessary.

The data list must have explicit consent from the data subjects. Article 5(2).

Reasonable due diligence of the data must be done prior to purchase.

Consent must be checked and validity obtained on:

How, When, and Who collected the list.

Someone other than the organisation doing the marketing because this is considered to be indirect consent and is not acceptable.

Note:

The 'soft opt-in' exception for emails or text marketing

<u>cannot</u> apply to contacts on a bought-in list.

A 'suppression list' should be maintained of people who have opted out or have told the business directly that they do not want to receive marketing.

Note:

Best practice - inform the individuals where their details have come from and ask if they want to withdraw consent, from other organisations as well. If so, inform the source that consent has been withdrawn from all users.

The Payment Card Industry Data Security Standard (PCI DSS) is an industry security standard designed to ensure that all companies that accept, process, store or transmit credit card information maintain a secure environment.

All security certificates must be kept up to date.

Payment system must be secure and robust.

Transparent processing and retention policy must be in place.

Clear refund policy information provided.

Automated Payments Collection

A website <u>must</u> be hosted with:

Secure **PCI DSS compliant hosting provider** in order to:

Accepts card payment

Processes card payment

Transmits cardholder data

Stores cardholder data

THREATS

Non-compliance with GDPR breaks the law.

Non-compliance is a **threat** to:

<u>All</u> businesses that handle the data of European citizens.

<u>All</u> Data Controllers and Processors who are unaware that they are held accountable and responsible for the personal data they process.

Breach of data:

A breach is a risk that must be communicated to the ICO and the data subject:

It must be reported within 72 hours. Articles 33-34.

There is a two-tiered sanction regime under GDPR:

Lesser incidents of non-compliance subject to a

maximum fine of €10 million

(£7.9 million) or 2% of turnover (whichever is greater).

The most serious violations could result in fines up to €20

million or 4% of annual turnover, whichever is greater.

Article 83(5).

The Information Commissioner's Office can also take enforcement action for non-compliance with direct marketing laws and selling marketing lists without people's knowledge or consent. Any breach of the DPA or PECR could result in an Enforcement Notice i.e. civil monetary penalties (fines) of up to £500,000.

ICO enforcement powers and policies are targeted and risk driven in line with:

Data Protection Regulatory Action Policy

Statement on enforcing the revised Privacy and Electronic Communications Regulations and guidance about the issue of monetary penalties.

The Threats can be reduced if:

A breach includes who is responsible for reporting the breach.

Details of the breach include when and how the data subject is informed.

The breach is reported within 72 hours. Article 33.

A disaster recovery plan is created.

Data collection is limited to what is <u>necessary</u> and <u>proportionate</u> for business purpose.

Controllers and processors are made aware that they are responsible and accountable for the personal data they process.

Security and safeguarding procedures for processing are implemented.

Any arrangements to transfer data to a third party outside of the arrangements identified in the GDPR are regarded as illegal.

Certification/ Code of Conduct is signed up to and followed.

The data subject rights are respected. Articles 15-22.

Explicit consent must be obtained to process personal data for one or more specified purposes for special categories of personal data. Article 9.

Processes, products and services must have a legal basis

and fulfil one or more specific requirements for the processing to be legal.

Data collected is adequate, relevant and limited to what is necessary in relation to the purposes for processing ('data minimisation'). Article 5(1c).

Conditions of consent must be acknowledged *European Directive 95/46/EC* in order to use personal data for marketing or use by others. ICO, *Direct Marketing.*

Appropriate technical and organisational measures are implemented to create 'privacy by design'. Article 25.

The **Privacy Policy** on your website must be easy to understand and explains how you will collect and process the data in accordance with the subject's GDPR Rights, Articles (12-22) and GDPR Principles, Articles 5-11.

Explain your Privacy policy.

How the data will be:

Accessed

Rectified

Transferred

Erased

Retained

Safeguarded

Stored

Shared

Used in automated decision making and profiling. ICO,

Privacy notices, transparency and control.

Subject Access Request (SAR):

Is a Right of Access by the data subject. Article 15.

What your data subjects can expect you to do and by when.

SAR must be made available within one (1) month from request.

Data subjects have a right to data portability, which should be provided in a commonly used and machine-readable format. Article 20.

The data collection method you will use must be made clear.

Automated system should be able to:

Easily track information

Delete the data when necessary/ acknowledge the Right to Erasure ('right to be forgotten'). Data subjects must be given the opportunity to be wiped from your system.

Article 17.

Implement a Data Protection Impact Assessment (PIA).

Article 35.

Classify all of the data you hold.

Do an inventory (data map).

Assign the appropriate data risk protection profiles.

Summary

When all of your policies, procedures, and protocols show that you understand **EU Citizens are the new data owners**, you will surely succeed with the GDPR. Data Protection by Design can benefit you because it is instrumental in helping people gain the confidence to entrust their data to you. The size of the effort you put into your GDPR compliance strategy and the amount of risk you assume is always an individual matter. But remember that GDPR compliance is worth considering very carefully. It will not only determine your legal compliance but also reveal how trustworthy your website/business will appear to be. The level of compliance chosen will clearly show how you regard personal data protection and will also reveal the value you place upon your relationships now and in the future. It sends a strong signal that shows how serious you are about your responsibility to protect the information of individuals and respect their rights.

Get a GDPR Compliance Health Check:

A preliminary assessment of your current level of preparedness for GDPR.

Pointers to guidance, models and good practice resources relevant to your needs.

Act Now!

Email: whitepritchard@website-wealth.uk

"The readiness is all." Shakespeare"

Preparing for the General Data Protection Regulation (GDPR)

12 Steps To Take Now

Awareness

Information You Hold

Communicating Privacy Information

Individuals' Rights

Subject Access Requests (SAR)

Lawful Basis For Processing Personal Data

Consent

Children

Data Breaches

Data Protection By Design and Data Protection Impact Assessments

Data Protection Officer

International

https://ico.org.uk/media/for-organisations/documents/1624219/preparing-for-the-gdpr-12-steps.pdf

The Rights

The Right To Be Informed

The Right To Access

The Right To Rectification

The Right To Erasure

The Right To Restrict Processing

The Right To Data Portability

The Right To Object

Rights In Relation To Automated Decision Making And Profiling

The Seven Principles

(for Data Controllers & Data Processors)

Principles relating to processing of personal data

Lawfulness of processing

Conditions of consent

Conditions applicable to child's consent in relation to
information society services

Processing of special categories of personal data

Processing of personal data relating to criminal
convictions and offences

Processing which does not require identification

The GDPR: Index of The Regulation

Chapter I – General provisions

1 Subject-matter and objectives

2 Material scope

3 Territorial scope

4 Definitions

Chapter II – Principles

5 Principles relating to processing of personal data

6 Lawfulness of processing

7 Conditions of consent

8 Conditions applicable to child's consent in relation to information society services

9 Processing of special categories of personal data

10 Processing of personal data relating to criminal convictions and offences

11 Processing which does not require identification

Chapter III – Rights of the data subject

Section 1 – Transparency and modalities

12 Transparent information, communication and modalities for the exercise of the rights of the data subject

Section 2 – Information and access to personal data

13 Information to be provided where personal data are collected from the data subject

14 Information to be provided where personal data have not been obtained from data subject

15 Right of access by the data subject

Section 3 – Rectification and erasure

16 Right to rectification

17 Right to erasure (right to be forgotten)

18 Right to restriction of processing

19 Notification obligation regarding rectification or erasure of personal data or restriction of processing

20 Right to data portability

Section 4 – Right to object and automated individual decision-making

21 Right to object

22 Automated individual decision-making, including profiling

Section 5 – Restrictions

23 Restrictions

Chapter IV – Controller and processor

Section 1 – General obligations

24 Responsibility of the controller

25 Data protection by design and by default

26 Joint controllers

27 Representatives of controllers or processors not established in the Union

28 Processor

29 Processing under the authority of the controller or processor

30 Records of processing activities

31 Cooperation with the supervisory authority

Section 2 – Security of personal data

32 Security of processing

33 Notification of a personal data breach to the supervisory authority

34 Communication of a personal data breach to the data subject

Section 3 – Data protection impact assessment and prior consultation

35 Data protection impact assessment

36 Prior consultation

Section 4 – Data protection officer

37 Designation of the data protection officer

38 Position of the data protection officer

39 Tasks of the data protection officer

Section 5 – Codes of conduct and certification

40 Codes of conduct

41 Monitoring of approved codes of conduct

42 Certification

43 Certification bodies

Chapter V – Transfer of personal data to third countries or international organisations

44 General principle for transfers

45 Transfers of the basis of an adequacy decision

46 Transfers subject to appropriate safeguards

47 Binding corporate rules

48 Transfers or disclosures not authorised by Union law

49 Derogations for specific situations

50 International cooperation for the protection of personal data

Chapter VI – Independent supervisory authorities

Section 1 – Independent status

51 Supervisory authority

52 Independence

53 General conditions for the members of the supervisory authority

54 Rules on the establishment of the supervisory authority

Section 2 – Competence, tasks and powers

55 Competence

56 Competence of the lead supervisory authority

57 Tasks

58 Powers

59 Activity reports

Chapter VII – Cooperation and consistency

Section 1 – Cooperation

60 Cooperation between the lead supervisory authority

and other supervisory authorities concerned

61 Mutual assistance

62 Joint operations of supervisory authorities

Section 2 – Consistency

63 Consistency mechanism

64 Opinion of the Board

65 Dispute resolution by the Board

66 Urgency procedure

67 Exchange of information

Section 3 – European Data Protection Board

68 European Data Protection Board

69 Independence

70 Tasks of the Board

71 Reports

72 Procedure

73 Chair

74 Tasks of the Chair

75 Secretariat

76 Confidentiality

Chapter VIII – Remedies, liabilities and penalties

77 Right to lodge a complaint with a supervisory authority

78 Right to an effective judicial remedy against a supervisory authority

79 Right to an effective judicial remedy against a controller or processor

80 Representation of data subjects

81 Suspension of proceedings

82 Right to compensation and liability

83 General conditions for imposing administrative fines

84 Penalties

Chapter IX – Provisions relating to specific processing situations

85 Processing and freedom of expression and information

86 Processing and public access to official documents

87 Processing of the nation identification number

88 Processing in the context of employment

89 Safeguards and derogations relating to processing for archiving purposes in the public interest, scientific or historical research purposes or statistical purposes

90 Obligation of secrecy

91 Existing data protection rules of churches and religious associations

Chapter X – Delegated acts and implementing acts

92 Exercise of the delegation

93 Committee procedure

Chapter XI – Final provisions

94 Repeal of Directive 95/46/EC

95 Relationship with Directive 2002/58/EC

96 Relationship with previously concluded Agreements

97 Commission reports

98 Review of other Union legal acts on data protection

99 Entry into force and application

References

Information Commission's Office, *Overview of the General Data Protection Regulation (GDPR)*
Information Commission's Office (ICO), *Subject Access Code of Practice*
Information Commission's Office (ICO), *Direct Marketing*
Information Commission's Office (ICO), *Conducting Privacy Impact Assessments*
Information Commission's Office (ICO), *Privacy notices, transparency and control*
ICO/ EU open source documents, Under the Open

Government Licence

http://www.legislation.gov.uk/ukpga/1998/29/contents

http://www.fairdata.org.uk/why-fair-data/

https://www.youtube.com/watch?v=WgVPylVy4sY&t=22s
https://ico.org.uk/media/for-organisations/documents/1624219/preparing-for-the-gdpr-12-steps.pdf

The Author

M White-Pritchard is a Certified GDPR Data Protection Officer (DPO General Data Protection Regulation) with many years of business experience in the private/public sectors and presently provides consultation to sole traders, micro, and SME businesses to ensure that online data protection practices are GDPR compliant.

Get a GDPR Compliance Health Check:

A preliminary assessment of your current level of preparedness for GDPR.

Pointers to guidance, models and good practice resources relevant to your needs.

Act Now!

Email: whitepritchard@website-wealth.uk

"The readiness is all." Shakespeare"